A STROKE, A SAVIOR, AND SURRENDER

The Day I Became a Survivor

Amy Tisdale

ISBN: 979-8-9987905-7-7(paperback)
Printed in the United States of America

Dedication:

*For my family-
who stayed, who carried me,
and who reminded me
that love does not leave
when life changes.*

*To the medical teams
who answered my never-ending
questions and worked tirelessly
to give me my life back.*

*And for every survivor,
learning how to live again.*

Special Thanks

This book exists because people showed up when I could not.

To my husband, Matt:
>   Who spoke when I could not, decided when I could not understand, and carried what no one should have to carry alone. Thank you for choosing me again and again in the moments that mattered most.

To our son, Caleb:
>   Whose courage, patience, and love anchored me more than he will ever know. You gave me reason to fight and grace when I could not be who I was before.

To our daughter, Rebecca:
>   Who met this season with strength beyond her years, and whose presence, patience, and love were a steady reminder of what mattered most. You gave me hope in quiet ways you may never fully realize. Who knew that nursing degree would matter so much just one year later...

To my family and closest friends:
>   Who stayed when life became complicated, who asked questions, showed up, waited, and never treated my healing like a deadline. Thank you for letting me be human.

To the medical professionals whose skill and vigilance gave me time:

To Dr. Shakir, Neurosurgeon,
> Thank you for your decisiveness, precision, and care when minutes mattered and outcomes were uncertain. Your willingness to listen and answer EVERY question has not gone unnoticed.

To Dr. Sidorov, Dr. Verma, and the neurology team:
> Thank you for your clarity, honesty, and commitment to doing what was necessary, even when it was hard to hear.

To Dr. Sanclement, ENT:
> Thank you for your incredible work in reconstructing my head, even if it wasn't a beautiful or easy process.

To the Neuro ICU nursing and therapy staff:
> Thank you for watching when I could not, advocating when I had no voice, and treating me as a person, not a condition.

To the rehabilitation physicians, therapists, and specialists, including Aaron, Chris Joe, Suzie, Alicia, Jennifer, Meredith, Jenna, Daniel, Dana, Ethan, Veronica, Colleen, Paige, Shad, Courtney, Mike, Diane, Raini, Ashley, Tyler, and countless others:
> Thank you for believing progress was possible before I did, and for meeting me with patience on days when progress felt invisible.

For anyone I left off:
> It's not because you didn't make an impact: I cannot remember every person I encountered.

To every medical professional who answered my questions, explained the unexplainable, and stayed steady in the long middle:
> Your work gave me time. Time changed everything.

To the communities who adapted, included, and made space:

Thank you for proving that belonging is not dependent on ability.

And to every survivor, caregiver, and reader:

Thank you for trusting me with your presence as I tell this story.

I carry all of you with me.

Amy Tisdale

Surrender - a poem

I thought surrender meant the end,
a laying down, a closing door
but it was breath I didn't earn,
and strength that met me on the floor.

What broke did not define my worth,
what stayed became enough somehow.
I lost the life I planned back then,
but found His presence even now.

Author's Note

This book is not a testimony of instant healing.
It is a story of staying.
Staying awake when it would have been easier to sleep.
Staying faithful when outcomes were unclear.
Staying present in a body that no longer felt familiar.
I did not write this to explain suffering or to offer spiritual shortcuts. I wrote it because life doesn't always resolve the way we hope, and faith doesn't require pretending it does.
If you are reading this while navigating loss, disability, grief, or a season you did not choose, I want you to know this story was written with you in mind.
You do not have to rush your healing.
You do not have to minimize your pain.
You do not have to wait until everything is fixed to live with purpose.
This is not a story about returning to who I was.
It is a story about who I am becoming.
On purpose, for a purpose, even now.

Dear Reader,

Before you turn the page, I want you to know something important.

This story contains challenging moments. Fear. Loss. Uncertainty. It also contains faith, but not the polished kind that skips over suffering.

If you are looking for a book that promises everything will be restored exactly as it was, this may not be it.

But if you are looking for honesty, presence, and hope that does not depend on outcomes, then you are in the right place.

You don't need to read this quickly.

You don't need to relate to every chapter.

You don't need to have the same beliefs to find meaning here.

All you need is permission to stay with your own story while you walk through mine.

Thank you for being here.

~Amy

1

Two Weeks After Surgery

Two weeks after surgery, life looked ordinary again.

That's what made it dangerous.

The headaches never stopped. Sharp. Constant. Unrelenting. They didn't ebb or fade or respond to medication. They sat behind my eyes and along my skull like a pressure that refused to loosen its grip.

Still, they had an explanation.

I wasn't scared, as I had had this procedure done two years prior. This "routine" surgery was supposed to be outpatient, but a bleeding complication led to an overnight stay, two weeks of massive headaches resulting in multiple contacts with my doctor and emergency room visits. The bleeding during the surgery had taken time to control. The doctors said irritation was expected - from the procedure itself, from what my body had been through. Pain doesn't always mean something is wrong. Sometimes it just means healing is slow, yet happening.

I believed that.

That Sunday evening felt normal. Friends had joined us for dinner, and afterward, I settled into the recliner to watch Sunday night football. I wasn't really watching; I was letting the familiar noise fill the room while I rested. Everything felt quiet. Manageable.

I reached for the handle to adjust my seat.

My left arm didn't move. I tried again. Nothing.

There was no pain beyond the headache already pounding through my head. No dizziness. No dramatic warning. Just a strange stillness, as if my body hadn't received the message my brain sent.

I waited, expecting it to catch up.

It didn't.

I didn't panic. I didn't feel afraid. I just sat there, staring at my arm as if it belonged to someone else, willing it out loud to respond. Surely this was temporary. Numbness. Fatigue. Something explainable.

When my husband walked in from outside, I spoke without thinking. Something ordinary. A simple sentence.

The words came out wrong.

Slurred. Heavy. Unfamiliar.

He stopped. Not just the kind of pause people make when they're confused, but the kind that comes from recognition. His eyes searched my face, taking in details I wasn't yet able to see.

"Amy," he said, already reaching for his phone. He told the dispatcher I was having a stroke.

I told him he was wrong. We didn't need *those people*—the paramedics—there. I insisted he hang up.

He wouldn't.

I didn't hurt. I was young. Strokes didn't happen like this. Not quietly. Not to people like me.

I remember feeling almost annoyed by his urgency. Embarrassed by it.

He didn't argue.

He simply took control to make sure I would be okay. He called friends to come be with our son, because we didn't know what was coming.

As he spoke, calm and direct, I sat there thinking how strange it was that everything still felt so ordinary. No collapse. No chaos.

Just a room that suddenly felt very still.

I didn't know then if he hadn't walked in,

If he hadn't recognized the signs-If I had gone to sleep instead of speaking

I likely wouldn't be here to tell this story.

But in that moment, all I knew was this:

Something had shifted.

And there was no going back.

2

Surely He's Wrong

I was sure my husband was overreacting.

I wasn't overly confused. I wasn't in pain, at least not in any new way. The headache was already there, sharp and relentless, but it had been there for days. This felt different. Smaller. Temporary.

I told him so.

I thought strokes didn't happen quietly. They didn't announce themselves with slurred words and a hand that wouldn't move while everything else stayed calm. They came with drama. With collapse. With chaos. With old age.

I didn't know the signs.

This felt inconvenient, not catastrophic.

He didn't raise his voice. He didn't panic. He didn't argue.

That scared me more than if he had.

When he spoke to the dispatcher, his tone was steady and urgent, the way it gets when something matters more than reassurance. I listened from the recliner, still trying to will my left hand into motion, still convinced that if I focused hard enough, my body would correct itself.

It didn't.

The minutes stretched. Too long. Long enough for doubt to creep in, not fear yet, but uncertainty. The kind that whispers, *What if this isn't nothing?*

I wanted to stand. To prove him wrong. To show that all of this was unnecessary.

I couldn't.

The headache pressed harder, a reminder that something had been wrong long before either of us realized the gravity of it.

The ambulance didn't arrive right away. The weather was bad. They were already on another call.

We waited.

I remember thinking how strange it was that time could slow down when it mattered most. How helpless it felt to know help was coming, and still be unable to make it arrive faster.

When the paramedics finally came, everything moved quickly and slowly at the same time. Questions. Lights. Voices I didn't recognize. Hands checking, lifting, assessing.

Our friends were there to steady us and to be with our son as the looming chaos settled in.

The paramedics spoke to my husband more than to me.

I didn't understand that.

I was still here. Still aware. Still myself. But my words weren't clear anyway.

But I could feel something shifting, not just in my body, but in how the room responded to me, as if control had already begun to slip away.

They loaded me into the ambulance and closed the doors.

The last thing I remember before we pulled away was the fear on my son's face and the quiet encouragement from my friend. I knew then that I wasn't facing this alone.

As we pulled away from the house, I stared at the ceiling and tried to pray. But the words wouldn't come, not because I didn't believe them, but because I didn't yet know what I was asking for.

I wasn't ready to think about what might be happening.

I just knew this wasn't how the day was supposed to go.

And for the first time, the thought crept in quietly and uninvited:

What if he isn't wrong?

3

Closest Hospital

The ambulance didn't take me where I would have chosen.

It took me to the closest hospital.

At the time, I didn't question that. I didn't yet understand how much geography could matter when minutes were already slipping away. I just knew the sirens were on, the lights were flashing, and my body was no longer mine to manage.

My husband wasn't in the ambulance with me. He followed behind.

I remember the doors closing. The motion. The ceiling above me. After that, everything blurs.

At the first hospital, the emergency room moved quickly. Tests. Scans. Conversations just outside my reach. At some point, the word I had been resisting finally landed.

Stroke.

There was a clot. Surgery was needed. Immediately.

But there was no neurosurgeon available that night.

As my husband settled at my bedside after initial tests, decisions were already being made. Calls placed. Arrangements finalized. The word *transfer* spoken as though it were simple.

It wasn't.

I don't remember the transfer to the second hospital.

I don't remember meeting the neurosurgeon.

I don't remember being told what would happen next.

Those details were given to my husband instead, because by the time I arrived, I was no longer able to carry them myself.

When I reached the second hospital, my husband and our daughter were there. From that moment on, Matt never left my side except when he was forced to.

He listened as the doctors explained what needed to happen. He heard the risks. The urgency. The uncertainty. He carried every detail I could not.

While I was taken into surgery, he was sent to a waiting room, where our daughter sat with him, trying to comfort him as they were unsure what the next moments would hold.

I don't remember the surgeon's face. I don't remember consent forms or final explanations. I don't remember being wheeled down long hallways or positioned under bright lights.

What I remember is surrender without ceremony.

My body was carried forward without my permission or my understanding, and the man who loved me most was left behind waiting, praying, hoping that the next update wouldn't be the one that shattered everything.

By the time I was taken away, the outcome was no longer in our hands.

And whether I woke up or not depended entirely on what happened next.

4

Still There

My first memory after arriving at the hospital was in the Neuro ICU. It wasn't pain.

It was being watched.

A team of doctors stood at the foot of my bed, their faces serious, attentive, searching. I didn't yet understand why they were there or what they were looking for. I only knew that their eyes were fixed on me, waiting for something.

Waiting for *me*.

The room felt foreign. Too bright. Too quiet in the way only ICU rooms are, machines humming softly, numbers blinking, time measured in beeps instead of minutes. My body felt heavy, uncooperative, like it belonged to someone else.

I was aware before I was oriented.

Aware that something big had happened.

Aware that I was being evaluated.

Aware that this moment mattered.

Someone asked me a question. I don't remember what it was, only the feeling that came with it. The sense that I was being invited back into the room. Back into myself.

So, I did the only thing that felt natural.

I made a joke.

It wasn't clever. It wasn't polished. It was instinctive, the reflex of a person who had always used humor to connect, to ease tension, to say *I'm here* without needing to explain it.

The response was immediate.

Faces softened. Smiles broke through the clinical focus. A ripple of relief moved through the room, unspoken but unmistakable.

She's still there.

I could feel it in the shift of energy. In the way shoulders relaxed in the excitement that followed, as if something fragile had just been confirmed.

I didn't fully understand what they had been worried about. Not yet. But I understood this much:

They weren't just checking my body.

They were checking *me*.

That joke, small and fleeting as it was, became evidence. Proof that I was still thinking. Still responding. Still myself.

Later, I would learn how close the line had been. How much uncertainty hung over those early moments. How carefully every word, every response, every movement had been measured.

But in that moment, all I knew was that laughter had found its way into the room.

And for the first time since everything had gone dark, I felt something stir beneath the exhaustion and confusion.

I was still here.

Not whole.

Not unchanged.

But present.

And that mattered more than I could have known.

5

Probably

The doctors didn't say it all at once.

It came in pieces, layered between scans and exams, folded into careful language meant to prepare rather than alarm. I was awake enough to understand but not awake enough to protect myself from the weight of what they were saying.

They talked about damage.
About swelling.
About what the brain does when blood flow is interrupted, and pressure rises where there is nowhere left to go.

They talked about my left side.

They said my left arm and hand would probably never be functional again.

Probably.

They said I might never walk without some kind of assistance.

Might.

They spoke the way professionals do: measured, calm, not unkind. They weren't predicting failure. They were explaining likelihood and preparing us for what was most realistic.

Still, the words landed like absolutes.

15

I tried to move my arm again, the way I had been doing since I woke up. I willed it to respond, to prove them wrong before the sentence was even finished. Nothing happened. My hand lay still, unfamiliar, as if it belonged to someone else.

I had lived my whole life without thinking about what it meant to reach for something. To walk across a room. To open a door. To hold a child's hand. These were not skills I had ever counted. They were assumptions.

And suddenly, they were all in question.

No one said the word *disability*, but it hovered in the room anyway. It was present in the pauses before answers, in the careful explanations of therapy rather than timelines. The way the doctors spoke to my husband was to make sure he understood what these probabilities could mean in the long term.

I watched his face as they spoke. He listened closely, storing information he would need to carry for both of us. He asked questions I hadn't thought to ask yet. He stayed steady when I couldn't.

I felt exposed in a way I never had before. My body was no longer private. My future was being discussed like a case file. I understood why it was necessary, but that didn't make it easier to hear my life reduced to likelihoods.

Probably never.
Might not ever.

Those words settled quietly. Not like panic. Not like grief yet. More like recognition. Something fundamental had shifted.

I had survived. But survival was not the same as preservation.

Not long after that conversation, a woman I hadn't met before came into my room. She introduced herself as the hospital social worker.

Her voice was gentle. Practiced. The kind of calm that comes from having had this conversation many times before, even though it was the first time it had ever been spoken over me.

She pulled a chair close to the bed and asked how I was feeling. I didn't know how to answer that anymore.

She told me she was there to help us navigate what came next.

Paperwork.
Resources.
Planning.

Then she said the words that settled more heavily than anything else that day.

Because of the extent of my injuries, she explained, I would qualify for disability benefits.

She paused before continuing.

Because, medically speaking, I was considered permanently disabled.

Permanently.

The word felt final in a way nothing else had yet. *Probably* had left room. *Might* had allowed breath. *Permanent* sounded like a door closing somewhere I couldn't see.

I stared at her badge while she spoke, watching the way it caught the light, because if I looked directly at her face, I thought I might break apart completely.

She explained the process carefully - forms, documentation, timelines, reassessments. She spoke kindly. Clearly. As if she were handing me a map.

But all I could hear was the destination.

Disability.

I had never imagined myself needing that word, never pictured my name attached to it. I had always been capable. Independent. Strong in ways that never required explanation.

And now someone was helping me plan for a life defined, at least on paper, by what I could no longer do.

It felt like grief wearing the disguise of help.

My husband asked practical questions. Thoughtful ones. I watched him absorb yet another future he hadn't chosen but was already carrying with care.

I nodded when appropriate. I listened. I tried to be cooperative, grateful even. I understood the necessity of what she was doing.

Still, it hurt.

When she left, I stared at my left hand again. The same hand that hadn't responded earlier. The same hand now carrying a label I wasn't ready to accept.

Permanent.

I didn't know then that permanence in medicine doesn't always mean finality in life. I didn't know how much could change, or how fiercely the human brain can fight when given time and repetition and grace.

All I knew in that moment was that the future I had assumed was gone, and the new one was being introduced with forms and definitions while I was still learning how to sit up on my own.

This was no longer just about surviving.

It was about learning how to live inside a body that might never fully return to me.

And that was harder to hear than anything else so far.

6

Room to Live

I didn't know I was fighting for my life.

Not really.

I knew I was being watched. I knew the scans mattered. I knew the doctors spoke carefully, choosing words that sounded calm even as their eyes tried to hide deep concern.

What I didn't know was that my brain was running out of room.

The swelling hadn't stopped. It was pressing, slowly but relentlessly, against the limits of my skull. The midline they had been watching so closely was no longer just something to monitor.

It was something that could decide whether I lived.

That part of the conversation didn't happen with me.

It happened with my husband.

He was told that if my brain didn't have room to swell, I would not survive. That waiting was no longer an option, that the next step was drastic, terrifying, and necessary.

A craniotomy.

They would remove a portion of my skull to relieve the pressure. Give my brain space to do what it needed to save my life.

He had to give consent.

While I lay in my ICU bed, still making jokes, still answering questions, still believing I was somewhere in the middle of recovery, the person I trusted most was being asked to decide whether to let surgeons open my head.

I didn't hear the risks explained.

I didn't hear the probabilities.

I didn't hear how uncertain the outcome still was.

He did.

He carried every word.

When it was time, the room shifted.

The steady rhythm of ICU, machines, familiar faces, quiet vigilance, gave way to movement. Purpose. Finality. People preparing me to leave the place that had come to feel safe.

As they began to wheel me out, my husband leaned close.

His voice didn't shake.

"Fight," he told me. "I still need you."

That was it.

Not a speech.

Not a promise.

Not a goodbye.

A plea.

I didn't understand the full weight of what he was saying. I didn't know how close the edge was, or how much he was holding together in that moment.

But I knew *him*.

I knew the way his voice sounded when something mattered more than anything else.

And somehow, even without understanding the battle ahead, I understood this:

I was needed.

As the doors closed behind us and the ICU disappeared from view, I left knowing less than everyone around me, but carrying one clear instruction.

Fight.

Even if I didn't know what I was fighting.

7

Taken Without Asking

I didn't wake up knowing what had been done.

I woke up knowing something was missing.

The first sensation wasn't pain, it was absence. A strange lightness where weight should have been. My head felt wrong, uneven in a way I couldn't yet explain.

The room came into focus slowly. Machines. Beeping. The familiar hum of the Neuro ICU returning but altered. Changed.

So was I.

I lifted my hand, my right one, and reached toward my head. Before I could touch anything, someone gently stopped me. A quiet instruction. A warning wrapped in care.

That's when it registered.

My hair was gone.

Not thinned. Not trimmed. Gone.

Shaved clean by a razor I hadn't asked for. A decision made while I was unconscious, necessary for the surgery, they would later tell me. Practical. Standard.

But no one had told *me*.

I knew, rationally, that this surgery had been urgent. That my life had been at risk. That there hadn't been time for preferences or permissions, the way there might have been before.

Still, the loss landed hard.

It wasn't vanity.

It was agency.

Another choice removed. Another part of myself altered without my voice in the room.

The craniotomy had saved my life. They had removed a portion of my skull to give my brain room to swell, to keep it from pressing against itself, to keep me alive.

I understood that.

What I wasn't prepared for was the way survival kept asking for pieces of me in return.

Hair grows back, people like to say.

And it does.

But in that moment, it felt like one more thing taken in a season already full of taking. One more reminder that my body was no longer mine to manage or protect.

When my husband came in, I saw his eyes search my face, not for fear this time, but for recognition. For reassurance that I was still here. Still me.

I wanted to tell him I was fine.

Instead, tears slipped before words could form.

He didn't try to explain it away. He didn't minimize it or rush me past it. He just stayed. Present. Steady. Letting grief have its space.

Later, someone would explain the bone flap, how it had been carefully removed and stored, how it would be put back once the swelling subsided and my body was ready for it.

Later, I would learn how many more surgeries were waiting ahead of me.

But in that moment, all I could feel was the truth settling in:

Survival had a cost.

And it was being paid in ways I never imagined.

8

The Mirror

I don't remember deciding to look.

I just remember suddenly being there caught by a reflection I wasn't prepared for.

It might have been a mirror. It might have been a photo. I'm not sure. What I know is that it didn't feel gradual. It felt like impact.

My head was shaved. Not neatly. Not stylish. Just bare and exposed, the skin unfamiliar, my scalp no longer something I recognized as mine. Staples and stitches traced lines I didn't yet know the story of. Evidence of how far surgeons had gone to save my life.

My face looked wrong.

One side drooped, subtle but unmistakable. My skin wasn't vibrant. It looked dull, almost lifeless, like it had forgotten how to glow. The woman staring back at me felt older, altered, stripped of something essential.

I stared, trying to make sense of what I was seeing.

This was the body that survived.

This was the body everyone kept calling a miracle.

And yet I felt devastated.

No one tells you that survival can come with grief. That waking up alive doesn't guarantee you'll recognize yourself. The first thing you might mourn isn't what you lost in the crisis, but what you see afterward.

I wanted to look away. To pretend I hadn't seen it. But the image stayed with me, settling into places I didn't yet have language for.

I wasn't afraid of being alive.

I was afraid of being *this*.

The machines continued their steady rhythm behind me, indifferent to my reflection. Nurses moved in and out, skilled and kind, treating my body as if it were familiar to them, something they understood.

Something I didn't.

I felt exposed in a way I had never felt before. Not just physically, but emotionally. Spiritually. Like everything I used to hide behind had been peeled away.

Hair. Symmetry. Strength.

Gone, altered, or uncertain.

I wondered, quietly and guiltily, if I was allowed to feel this way - if gratitude was supposed to cancel out grief. If being alive meant I shouldn't mourn what had changed.

But lying there, faced with a version of myself I didn't recognize, I couldn't separate the two.

I was grateful.

And I was heartbroken.

Both were true.

And neither canceled the other.

9

Why This Path

I had always believed God was purposeful.

I believed He was intentional, attentive, and involved. I believed that even when things hurt, there was meaning somewhere beneath the surface, a reason I might not see yet, but one I trusted existed.

Lying in that hospital bed, I wanted to know why this path was mine.

Not in a poetic way. Not in a sermon-ready way. I wanted to know why *this* body, *this* brain, *and this* life had been interrupted so completely. Why the story I thought I was living had been rewritten without my consent.

People spoke around me with confidence. They said things like *God has a plan* and *He's not finished yet*. I knew they meant well. I knew those words had carried me before.

But now, they felt distant, like truths I believed in theory but couldn't yet reach in practice.

I wasn't angry with God. Not exactly. I just couldn't reconcile Him with what had happened.

If He was good, why this much loss?
If He were sovereign, why this kind of interruption?
If He loved me, why did survival come at such a high cost?

I didn't speak those questions aloud. They felt too sharp. Too irreverent. I had spent my life trusting God; I didn't want to sound like someone who suddenly didn't.

So, I asked them quietly, inside myself, where no one else could hear.

Why me.
Why now.
Why this way.

Faith, I was learning, doesn't disappear in suffering. It just becomes heavier to carry.

I still prayed. But my prayers weren't eloquent. They weren't hopeful. Most of the time, they were just a sentence long.

I don't understand.
This hurts.
Please don't leave me here like this.

I didn't need answers yet. I just needed to know that God could sit with questions He didn't immediately resolve.

10

I'm Not Done Living

It was said casually.

Not cruelly. Not with malice. Just matter-of-fact, as if the conclusion had already been drawn and everyone but me had accepted it.

A nurse at inpatient rehab looked surprised when she realized I was being discharged home instead of transferred to a nursing home. Her reaction was immediate and unfiltered - shock, followed by confusion. As if my going home didn't quite make sense given the condition of my body and my abilities.

I didn't argue with her. I didn't have the strength.

But the moment she left the room, the weight of her surprise settled heavily on my chest. Something inside me cracked open, and I began to sob.

I turned to Matt and said through tears, "That's where people go to die. And I'm not done living."

The words came out raw and desperate, fueled by fear I hadn't yet given language to. It wasn't that I believed every nursing home was a place without care or dignity. It was what it represented to me in that moment - finality. An unspoken agreement that my life had narrowed to maintenance instead of meaning.

I wasn't ready to accept that.

I knew my body was broken in ways it might never fully recover from. I knew life would look different. Harder.

33

Smaller in some ways. But I also knew this: my story wasn't finished. Not yet. Maybe not ever in the way others expected, but it wasn't over.

What shook me most wasn't the suggestion itself. It was the realization that others had already begun to imagine the limits of my future - quietly, without asking me if I agreed.

Matt didn't try to fix it. He didn't minimize my fear or offer false reassurance. He stayed with me in that moment, holding the weight of it with me, reminding me, without words, that choosing life sometimes looks like refusing to accept someone else's ending for your story.

Going home wasn't just about location.

It was about hope.

About autonomy.

About believing that life could still hold purpose, even if it required more effort, more help, and more grace than before.

That moment marked something important inside me. I didn't yet know how I would live in this changed body. I didn't know what recovery would demand. But I knew I wasn't ready to be placed somewhere my life would be quietly concluded.

I wasn't done living.

And as fragile as my body was, that truth felt stronger than anything I had lost.

I was forty-three years old. Too young to accept the quiet ending others seemed prepared to assign me. Too alive to believe my story had narrowed to a hallway and a call light. I didn't know how I would live in this changed body, or how much life it would demand from me, but I knew this, I wasn't done. Going home wasn't just a medical decision. It was a declaration. A refusal to let fear, assumptions, or prognosis define the boundaries of my future. And when the day finally came to leave, I carried that truth with me, fragile and fierce, as I crossed the threshold back into life.

11

The Weight I Carried

The hardest part wasn't the weakness.

It wasn't the slowness, the frustration, or the way my body refused to cooperate. Those things were visible. Tangible. Easy to name.

The hardest part was the weight of feeling like a burden.

Every movement required help. Someone had to adjust me, lift me, steady me, wait for me. My independence disappeared so quickly that it felt like it had been erased rather than lost.

I watched the people I loved rearrange their lives around my needs.

Appointments. Schedules. Conversations. Decisions. Everything bent in my direction, and I hated that I was the reason.

No one complained. No one made me feel unwanted. They showed up with patience and care, insisting I wasn't a problem to solve or an inconvenience to manage.

But inside, I felt heavy.

I measured myself by what I could no longer contribute, by the ways I slowed everyone down, by how much energy it took to include me in ordinary moments.

I didn't want to need this much.

I didn't want my husband to have to think for both of us.
I didn't want my children to see me like this.
I didn't want my presence to feel complicated.

I worried that love, over time, would turn into obligation. That patience would thin. That the weight I felt would eventually be felt by everyone else, too.

No one said those things. They didn't have to. My mind supplied them easily.

Needing help reshapes how you see yourself. It introduces questions you didn't know you'd ever ask.

Am I still useful?
Am I still wanted?
Am I worth the effort it takes to keep me included?

I knew, intellectually, that my value wasn't based on productivity. I had said that to others before. I believed it for them.

Believing it for myself was harder.

I tried to minimize my needs. I apologized too much. I thanked people excessively, as if gratitude could offset inconvenience.

I didn't realize then that carrying this shame was its own kind of weight, one that made healing heavier, not lighter.

I was learning how to survive in a body that needed help.

What I hadn't learned yet was how to let myself be carried without believing I was a burden.

That lesson would come later.

12

Held

Somewhere in those ICU days, before discharge was even discussed, there was a moment that grounded everything that followed. The ICU was quiet in the way sacred spaces often are.

Not silent, just hushed. Machines hummed softly. Monitors blinked and measured things I didn't fully understand. Time felt suspended, as if the world outside the room had agreed to wait.

My mom sat beside me.

She had been there through so much already, watching, praying, holding steady when nothing else felt steady. In that room, with its sterile light and constant vigilance, she felt like an anchor.

At my request, she had turned on worship music.

I remember the sound filling the space in a way that didn't feel intrusive. It felt invited.

Goodness of God began to play.

I had heard the song before, but this time it landed differently. Every word felt closer to the bone. Not abstract. Not poetic. Real. Earned. Tested.

As the music swelled, something in me stirred.

I lifted my right arm.

It wasn't dramatic. It wasn't strong. But it was intentional. A small act of worship offered with everything I had left. Tears slid down my face as the truth of the moment pressed in around me.

I wanted to lift both arms.

I couldn't.

At my request, my mom gently reached for my left arm and raised it for me.

Together, we worshipped like that, one arm mine, one arm held, my weakness carried by someone who loved me. My praise completed by grace.

In that moment, I didn't feel broken.

I felt held.

Held by my mother's steady hands.

Held by the music wrapping around the room.

Held by a God whose goodness hadn't disappeared just because my life no longer looked the way I expected.

I didn't know then how long the road ahead would be. I didn't know how much more loss, adjustment, or surrender would be required.

But I knew this:

I was not alone in the fight.

And even in a body that no longer worked the way it once had, even in a season I didn't understand, I could still worship.

That song became my anthem.

Not because everything was good.

But because **God was**.

And somehow, even there, that was enough to lift my arms.

13

Worth It

The days in the Neuro ICU began to blur together.

Light and dark mattered less than vitals and scans. Nurses rotated. Doctors checked in. Time was marked by medications, therapy visits, and the quiet hums and beeps of machines that never seemed to sleep.

My body was still healing. Still swollen. Still fragile.

But my mind was awake.

And my heart was wrestling with questions I didn't yet have answers for.

One day, my mom sat beside me, her presence steady in a way only a mother's can be. We talked quietly, carefully, about survival, about what happened, about how close everything had come to ending differently.

The words felt heavy in the air.

And somewhere in that conversation, I heard myself say it.

"If one person comes to know Christ through this, it will be worth it."

The sentence surprised me as much as it did her.

I don't know if I fully understood the weight of what I was saying in that moment. I don't think I grasped the long road ahead, the permanent changes, the losses that would keep unfolding long after the crisis passed.

What I did know was this:

My life had been spared.

And if it had a purpose beyond my own comfort, beyond returning to what had been, then I wanted to be open to that.

I wasn't bargaining with God.

I wasn't trying to make sense of suffering.

I was anchoring myself to meaning.

That statement wasn't bravado. It wasn't a spiritual performance. It was a quiet offering made from a hospital bed by someone who had just learned how fragile life really is.

I didn't yet know how many people would hear my story.

I didn't know how far it would reach.

I didn't know how much of myself I would have to give along the way.

I only knew that survival alone wasn't enough.

If I was still here, there had to be a reason.

And even now, looking back with more clarity than I had then, I can admit something gently and honestly:

I didn't understand the full cost of that prayer.

I didn't know yet how much surrender it would require.

But I meant it.

I still do.

Because purpose doesn't always arrive fully formed. Sometimes it begins as a single sentence whispered in faith before the outcome is clear.

And that sentence became a thread, one I would follow long after the ICU, long after the scars, long after life stopped looking the way it once had.

14

Learning Again

Eventually, the ICU gave way to another kind of room.

Less urgent. Less quiet. Less sacred in some ways; but no less difficult.

Inpatient rehab.

It didn't feel like progress at first. It felt like exposure. Like being moved from the place where everyone expected you to be fragile into a place where effort was required - measured, observed, repeated.

This was where healing stopped being theoretical.

This was where it became work.

Therapists introduced themselves and then introduced me to tasks I had once done without thought. Sitting up. Transferring and standing, even if only for a moment. Every movement was broken down into steps so small they felt insulting.

Until I realized they weren't.

They were necessary.

My body didn't remember what my mind knew. Signals misfired. Muscles stayed quiet when asked to engage. My left side felt distant, like it belonged to someone else and hadn't yet decided whether to cooperate.

Nothing happened quickly.

Nothing happened quietly.

Rehab was loud with effort. With frustration. With the constant reminder of what had been lost. With cries sounding like defeat. With success measured in inches. In seconds. In moments when something moved that hadn't moved before.

And in moments when it didn't.

I learned quickly that progress wasn't linear. A good day could be followed by a discouraging one. Gains could vanish overnight. Strength could feel present one moment and absent the next.

That was humbling.

I had been competent before. Capable. Independent. Now I needed help with things I never imagined I would need. And that kind of dependence reaches places pride likes to hide.

I cried more in rehab than I had in the ICU.

The ICU had been about staying alive. Rehab was about facing what life might look like now.

But something else happened there, too; something quieter.

Hope became practical.

Not the big, sweeping kind. Not the grandeur miracle kind. The kind that shows up in repetition. In small wins. In showing up again after a hard session because there was no other way forward.

I learned to celebrate effort, not outcome.

I learned that strength didn't always look like standing tall. Sometimes it looked like showing up exhausted and trying anyway.

I learned that surrender wasn't passive.

It was active.

It was choosing to engage even when the outcome was uncertain. It was trusting God not just with survival, but with the process.

Every day in rehab, I asked myself the same question:

Will you keep going?

And somehow, through frustration, tears, and moments of quiet resolve, I did.

Not because I was strong.

But because I was still here.

And that meant there was more to learn.

Another day, another challenge I didn't ask for.

During one inpatient therapy session, my therapist pointed to a small step inside the building, no bigger than most people would notice. He explained that we were going to practice navigating it, treating it like a curb.

I stared at it and felt my throat tighten. I froze.

That small rise might as well have been a mountain.

At that point, I could barely walk using a specialized cane. My balance felt fragile, unreliable. The idea of stepping up and over something, even something small, felt impossible. Tears filled my eyes as frustration and fear collided. How would I ever manage real curbs? Sidewalks? The world outside these walls?

I stood there crying, frozen by what felt insurmountable.

But my therapist didn't dismiss my fear. He didn't minimize it. He stood beside me and began to walk me through it, not just physically, but mentally. Step by step. Breath by breath. Where to place my foot. How to shift my weight. When to trust the movement.

And then I did it.

I stepped up.

I stepped over.

I stepped down.

It wasn't graceful. It wasn't easy. But it was real.

That moment taught me something more profound than balance or strength. It taught me that what looks impossible at first glance often becomes possible when someone walks patiently beside you and reminds you that you don't have to do it all at once.

15

Going Home

Going home was supposed to mean something.

After weeks of monitors, alarms, rounds, and waiting rooms, discharge felt like a word full of promise. I was still weak. Still healing. Still wearing a helmet everywhere I went because a piece of my skull was missing. But I was alive, and I was leaving the clinical setting. That felt like progress.

Home looked different from the way it used to. Furniture had been rearranged. Pathways widened. Ramps and grab bars installed. Everyday objects suddenly required intention. My world had become smaller and more deliberate, measured in steps and energy rather than hours and plans.

The helmet became part of me. It was uncomfortable and awkward, but it was also protection. A visible reminder that I was still vulnerable in ways no one could see just by looking at me. I wore it faithfully, knowing it stood between my fragile brain and the unpredictable nature of gravity. I lived with the fear of knowing a fall without it could be catastrophic.

There was relief in sleeping in my own bed, even when sleep came in fragments. Relief in familiar walls. Relief in quiet. Hospital life trains you to expect interruption; home gave me space to breathe again.

Home health nursing visits replaced hospital rounds. Medication schedules replaced IV drips. Healing, I assumed, had moved into a different phase, less dramatic, more routine. We were watching and waiting, doing exactly what we were told to do.

I wanted to believe the worst was behind us.

I had already survived what should have taken my life. I had endured surgeries, fear, and the unrelenting unknown. Surely this was the easier part now. Surely this was the season where my body would mend if given enough time.

There was still fear, of course. But it lived quietly beneath gratitude. I was home. That had to mean something.

16

When Healing Stalled

My husband noticed it before I did.

During a routine home nursing visit, he pointed it out to the nurse during her routine wound check. She paused while examining my scalp. Her hands lingered longer than they should have. Her voice changed, not alarmed, but serious. There was a darkened area that concerned her. She didn't speculate. She didn't reassure. She made the call that sent us back to see my neurosurgeon immediately.

What I thought was healing had been something else entirely.

Because of compromised blood flow from my earlier, yet very complicated, surgery, the skin over my surgical site had begun to die. The word necrotic was delivered carefully, clinically, as if gentleness could soften its meaning. Dead tissue. Tissue that could not recover.

The bone flap that had been replaced after my first surgery could not stay.

It would have to be removed again - another brain surgery.

This time, it wouldn't be saved. The flap was discarded as medical waste, gone permanently. A strange finality settled in that moment. Something that had once protected my brain, something that represented progress, was now irretrievable.

51

Once again, healing shifted beneath my feet.

My neurosurgeon worked closely with an ENT specialist to create a plan. The problem wasn't just replacing bone; it was whether my skin could support it. The solution would take time. Skin would need to be slowly stretched to prepare for what came next.

A custom, 3D-printed plate would eventually replace what had been lost.

Eventually.

The word hung in the air heavier than any diagnosis. There was no clear timeline. No neat progression. Only waiting. Again.

What I thought was a chapter of recovery turned out to be another lesson in patience. I survived the stroke. I survived surgery. I survived going home. But healing was not finished asking things of me.

I had no strength left to bargain with God. No energy to rewrite the story. All I could do was accept that this, too, was part of the path I hadn't chosen.

Once again, I placed my future in the hands I had no choice but to trust.

17

Leaving to Heal

Progress didn't mean staying close to home.

That realization came slowly, then all at once.

After research and meeting with doctors, we realized that if I wanted the best chance at regaining what had been lost, I would need to go somewhere else. A highly specialized stroke rehabilitation facility, one equipped for deficits like mine, one that could push me beyond maintenance and into possibility.

It meant leaving home. I chose to go while I was between surgical procedures.

Leaving familiarity.

Leaving comfort.

Leaving the rhythms that had already been disrupted too much.

Most painfully, it meant leaving my son who had just completed his Freshman year, one I spent in the hospital and in inpatient therapy, missing so many pivotal moments.

He was fourteen, old enough to understand, young enough to still need me in ways I couldn't explain or replace. And my daughter, grown now, with her own life and responsibilities, yet still my child in every way that mattered.

The decision felt cruel and necessary at the same time.

I wasn't choosing rehab over my family.

I was choosing it *for* them.

But knowing that didn't make it easier.

Packing for that move felt different than packing for surgery or a hospital stay. This wasn't about survival anymore. This was about separation. About trusting that love could stretch across distance the same way my body was being asked to stretch toward healing.

When it came time to leave, I held everything together until I couldn't anymore.

Goodbyes are hard under normal circumstances. These weren't normal. These were layered with uncertainty, no guarantees, no timelines, no promises about what I would come back with.

I didn't know what, or even if anything, I would regain.

I only knew what I was risking.

As I left, I carried guilt alongside hope. The kind of guilt that whispers you're choosing yourself when you should be choosing your children. The kind of hope that answers back, *This is how you choose them.*

The facility was impressive. Advanced. Focused. Everything about it said *this is where people come to work hard.* But it was also unfamiliar. Louder in a different way than hospitals are. Less comforting. More demanding. It didn't look like a hospital, it looked like a gym and LOTS of work!

Here, no one knew me as a mom or a wife.

They knew me as a patient.

As a body with deficits.

As a brain with damage.

As someone who needed to relearn.

I cried the first night in our temporary home.

Not because I didn't believe in what I was doing, but because believing didn't cancel the ache of being away from the people who anchored me.

Healing, I was learning, sometimes requires distance.

Not from love, but from comfort.

And choosing that kind of healing asks for a different kind of strength.

The kind that leaves home not because it wants to, but because it must.

There was a day in intensive rehab when my physical therapist asked me to let go. To this point, if out of my wheelchair, I had been walking with supporting hands, bars, anything solid enough to borrow confidence from. He first just wanted me to stand, then gently suggested I try a few steps on my own. The room felt suddenly too quiet. My heart pounded as fear rushed in faster than logic.

Not metaphorically. Physically.

Letting go felt reckless. Dangerous. I knew what my body couldn't do. I had lived inside its limits long enough to respect them. Standing there without support felt like stepping off a cliff and trusting the ground to appear.

But he didn't rush me. He stood close. He spoke calmly. He reminded me to breathe. And then, somehow, I took a step.

Then another.

And before I could even process what had happened, I was crying, the crying that comes when fear finally releases its grip and hope, along with joy, floods in all at once. My legs were shaking, my chest was heaving, and my heart felt too full for my body to contain.

My husband had stepped away for just a moment. I grabbed my phone with trembling hands and called him, telling him to come back immediately. When he returned and saw what had happened, we stood there together, both of us crying, rejoicing in what those steps meant.

They weren't just steps.

They were hope in motion.

18

The First Day

There was one date I would not surrender.

The first day of my son's Sophomore year.

I had never missed a first day of school. Not once. No matter what life looked like, I had always been there, watching backpacks disappear through doors, taking pictures I would save long after the years moved on.

I wasn't letting the stroke take that too.

When the rehabilitation coordinators talked about discharge timelines and treatment plans, I listened carefully. I understood the importance of structure, of consistency, of following protocol. I understood what they were trying to protect.

But I also knew what *I* needed to protect.

So I begged.

Not dramatically. Not angrily. Just honestly. I told them what that day meant. What it would cost me to miss it. How much of myself I had already given up, and how this mattered in a way no chart could capture.

I expected resistance.

Instead, I was met with something unexpected.

Flexibility with understanding.

They adjusted my treatment plan. Shifted schedules. Reworked goals. Not because I was being unreasonable, but because they recognized that healing isn't only physical.

Sometimes it's deeply personal.

The day I left didn't feel like an early discharge.

It felt like grace.

Every movement still took effort. Every task required intention. But beneath the exhaustion was relief, because I wasn't just going home for a moment.

I was going home.

Rehab wouldn't stop. It would continue there, through appointments, exercises, and the slow discipline of daily work. Healing would still be demanded of me, just in a different setting.

That August morning, as my son prepared for his first day of his Sophomore year of high school, I watched him with a heart fuller than it had ever been. He was taller. Older. Standing on the edge of something new.

And I was there.

Maybe not the way I had imagined years before. Maybe slower. Maybe seated. Maybe altered.

But present.

When the picture was taken, it captured more than a milestone. It captured resolve; a quiet refusal to let loss define everything that followed.

The stroke had taken so much.

But it had not taken this.

Because healing doesn't always mean leaving life behind to find yourself again.

Sometimes it means bringing the work home and choosing to keep showing up anyway.

19

Cone Head

The plan to stretch my skin required surgery to place a tissue expander. This couldn't happen until I returned home from the intense rehab hospital. The saline-filled balloon expander didn't just change my head.

It changed how I saw myself.

As fluid was added, my scalp stretched higher and tighter, reshaping my head into something unnatural. It wasn't subtle. It wasn't gradual enough to adjust to.

It turned me into a cone head.

There's no gentler way to say it.

My head rose sharply beneath my skin, distorted in a way that didn't look medical; it looked monstrous. Every accidental reflection confirmed what I already felt.

I felt hideous.

Not sick.

Not fragile.

Hideous.

This wasn't about vanity. It was about dignity. I had already lost my hair. My symmetry. My familiar face. Now even the shape of my head felt wrong, foreign, like something I couldn't mentally reconcile as me.

Each adjustment reminded me that my body was still under construction. Still being altered. Still not done.

That was when I knew I couldn't be seen like this.

So I covered it.

Chemo caps became my armor. Soft enough to make me feel human again. Neutral enough to keep questions away. They allowed me to move through public spaces without becoming a spectacle or an explanation.

I wasn't denying what had happened.

I was protecting myself while it was still happening.

By then, my scars weren't from one surgery. They were layered evidence of how many times my body had been opened in the name of survival.

Healing, I was learning, isn't just about what the body can endure.

It's about what the soul can tolerate.

And during that season, being seen like that was more than I could bear.

20

Seen

The first time I returned to church after that procedure, I tried to disappear.

I wore a chemo cap, hoping it might soften what was happening to my head. I wasn't wearing a helmet any longer as it wouldn't fit with the reconstructive work going on.

And I was still in a wheelchair since I did not yet have solid protection covering my brain, so every movement mattered. Every shift of my body was measured, supported, deliberate.

Church had always been a place of familiarity. Of comfort. Of shared faith and faces that knew me as I was before. Walking, or rather, being wheeled, into that space like this felt exposed in a way I wasn't prepared for.

I was acutely aware of how I looked.

A cone head covered by a chemo cap.

A wheelchair.

A body that moved differently.

And with that awareness came a quiet, gnawing fear:

What if they think I look ridiculous or have a mental disability too?

No one had said it. No one implied it. But fear doesn't wait for evidence. It fills in the gaps on its own. I worried people would look at me and assume my mind had been damaged along with my body, that I wasn't all there anymore.

That I wasn't *me*.

I knew I was present. I knew I was thinking clearly. But perception is powerful, and I couldn't control it.

As I sat there, surrounded by worship and familiar faces, I felt both seen and invisible at the same time, noticed for how I looked, but uncertain whether people still recognized who I was beneath it.

A woman came up to me, someone I knew, someone who meant no harm. Her voice was gentle. Her eyes were full of care.

"You look like you've really been through it," she said.

She meant it in love.

I know that now. I knew it then.

But the words still landed heavy.

Because she was right.

I *had* been through it and I couldn't hide it.

And suddenly, I fully realized my suffering, something I was still trying to understand privately, was visible to everyone else. Spoken out loud in a space where I had once felt effortlessly known.

I smiled. I nodded. I did what felt expected.

Inside, I wrestled with the reality that survival had changed how I entered rooms.

That day, I realized something important:

People didn't need details to know I had suffered.

They only needed to see me.

And I wasn't sure yet how to carry that.

The cap stayed on. The wheelchair stayed beneath me. And I sat there holding two truths at once:

I was still fully myself.

And I was no longer invisible.

It wasn't the concern that hurt. It was realizing how visible my suffering had become.

21

Help

Recovery didn't end when I came home.

In many ways, that's where it became most real.

For the first couple of months, therapy came to me. In-home sessions filled the spaces where everyday life used to live. Exercises happened in the living room. Progress was measured in familiar hallways. The place that had once meant rest and comfort became a training ground.

Healing moved in.

Even with therapy happening at home, I couldn't do everything on my own. Not safely. Not consistently. Not without exhausting myself or risking setbacks.

So we hired a daytime caregiver.

That decision carried more weight than I expected.

I had never needed help like that before. I had been capable. Independent. The one managing schedules, running errands, and showing up for everyone else.

Now I needed someone to help me get dressed. To assist with meals. To make sure I got where I needed to go, especially to appointments that seemed endless in those early months.

Therapy sessions. Follow-ups. Scans. Evaluations.

I wasn't just accepting help.

I was relinquishing control.

At first, it felt deeply uncomfortable. Embarrassing, even. There is a quiet grief that comes with realizing you can't meet your own basic needs the way you once did. No one prepares you for how much identity is wrapped up in independence.

Needing help made me feel exposed.

Not weak but changed.

My caregiver learned the rhythms of my days. The pace I needed. The moments when I pushed too hard and the moments when I needed encouragement to try again. She became part of the scaffolding holding my life upright while I rebuilt it piece by piece.

That took humility.

It also took trust.

As weeks passed, in-home therapy gave way to something new.

Outpatient therapy.

That transition felt significant; not because everything was suddenly easier, but because it marked movement. Forward motion. A shift from survival to sustained effort.

Getting to outpatient appointments required planning. Coordination. Help. But it also required resolve.

Each session asked something of me.

Focus. Patience. Willingness to fail in front of others and try again anyway.

I was learning that recovery isn't just about regaining function.

It's about learning how to live honestly in the in-between, where you're not who you were, but not yet who you're becoming.

Needing help didn't mean I was stuck.

It meant I was still moving.

Just not alone.

22

Still Included

After months of learning how to accept help and after returning home changed in ways I couldn't undo something unexpected happened.

There were things I knew I would miss.

Some of them were obvious, walking without thinking, moving without planning, doing things the way I always had. Others surprised me by how deeply they cut.

One of those centered around the marching band.

I had imagined being a fully involved marching band mom. The long nights. The practices. The performances. Being on the sidelines, cheering until my voice was gone. It was supposed to be a season of pride and presence, of showing up in ways that felt active and whole.

After the stroke, I couldn't do those things.

Not the way I had planned.

My body couldn't keep up with the pace. The physical demands were too much. The version of motherhood I had pictured, one that involved constant motion and independence, was no longer possible.

That loss was quieter than some of the others, but it was heavy.

It was another reminder that even good dreams can grieve you when they're taken away.

What I didn't expect was what happened next.

The other parents noticed.

Not in a way that made me feel pitied or singled out, but in a way that felt intentional. Thoughtful. Kind. They didn't try to fix my limitations or pretend they weren't there.

They simply asked how they could include me.

They stepped in so I could do what I could without feeling like a burden. They found ways to make space instead of excuses. Ways to help me feel I belong without apologizing for my needs.

Then came the performance.

A parent mini marching performance, something meant to be fun, lighthearted, communal. Something I assumed I would have to watch from the sidelines.

Instead, they invited me in.

They turned my wheelchair into a car.

Decorated it. Incorporated it. Made it part of the story instead of something to work around. They handed me a color guard flag and gave me a role that mattered, not symbolic, not token.

Real.

As the music played and we moved together, something inside me loosened.

I wasn't watching life happen from the outside.

I was in it.

Rolling. Smiling. Participating in a way that didn't ignore my reality but didn't diminish me either. They didn't ask me to pretend I wasn't disabled.

They made sure disability didn't mean exclusion.

That moment did more than include me in the performance.

It healed something.

It reminded me that community, at its best, doesn't ask you to keep up; it walks with you. It adapts. It makes room.

I had lost the version of motherhood I imagined.

But I was given something else in its place.

A front-row seat to grace.

23

Still Becoming

Early recovery didn't give me everything back.

That was a realization that arrived slowly, then settled in for good.

I can walk short distances now, with a cane. Every step is intentional. Measured. Earned. It's not the effortless movement I once took for granted, but it is movement. And I don't dismiss that.

My left arm, the one doctors warned might never regain function, surprised everyone.

Including me.

There is limited movement in my shoulder now. Small gains. Quiet victories. Nothing dramatic, but enough to remind me that predictions are not promises. That bodies can surprise. That healing doesn't always follow the neat lines we draw for it.

My hand, though, remains still.

It may never recover.

That truth is one I carry carefully. Some days with peace. Some days with grief. But always with faith that doesn't demand outcomes, only trust.

I was told many things in those early days about what would and wouldn't come back. I listened. I learned. But I also learned something else:

Doctors can speak to probability.

God still speaks to possibility.

I hold to both.

Around the same time my body was settling into what recovery would look like, my life expanded in another way.

I became a grandmother.

Joy arrived carrying grief with it.

I had imagined what kind of grandma I would be, the activities, the movement, the freedom. I had pictured myself doing the things I had once done so easily.

That version of grandmotherhood isn't mine.

And that loss matters.

I grieved it quietly, because joy doesn't erase disappointment. It simply learns to coexist with it. I can't do everything I dreamed of, but I still get to be a grandma.

I get to love.

I get to show up.

I get to be present in ways that don't always require physical strength to be meaningful.

There are moments when I watch from a chair instead of joining in. Moments when my body reminds me of its limits, just as my heart wants to leap past them.

And there are moments when gratitude floods in unexpectedly, because I am here. Because I am alive. Because I get to witness life continuing, even when it looks different from what I imagined.

Recovery didn't return me to who I was.

It introduced me to who I am becoming.

Still adapting.

Still learning.

Still holding grief and joy in the same hands.

I am not finished.

I am still becoming.

24

On Purpose

At some point, survival stopped being the question.

I was here.

That truth had settled in my bones long before I fully understood what it would require of me. I had lived through the surgeries, the uncertainty, the rehab, the grief of what didn't come back. I had learned how to move through the world differently.

The question that remained was quieter but heavier.

Why?

Not in an angry way. Not even in a desperate one. But in a way that asked for meaning beyond endurance.

I kept coming back to the same truth, over and over again:

God left me here on purpose for a purpose.

That didn't mean I understood the suffering. It didn't mean I could trace every loss back to a neat explanation. It simply meant that my life continuing was not an accident.

And if it wasn't an accident, then I didn't want to waste it.

I began to write.

At first, it wasn't for an audience. It was for survival. For processing. For naming things I didn't yet know how to say out loud. Words gave shape to experiences that felt too big to carry quietly.

Writing helped me make sense of the fracture between who I had been and who I was becoming.

It helped me grieve honestly.

It helped me notice grace.

It helped me tell the truth without rushing it toward resolution.

And then something unexpected happened.

Other people saw themselves in the words.

People reached out. Stroke survivors. Caregivers. Those navigating disability, grief, and faith in bodies that no longer worked the way they once had. They didn't want answers.

They wanted companionship.

They wanted honesty.

They wanted someone who didn't minimize the hard parts or rush them toward hope.

They wanted proof that life could still be meaningful, even when it looked nothing like the plan.

That's when advocacy began - not as a title, not as a platform, but as a response.

I started speaking up. Sharing what access really looks like. Naming the barriers people don't notice until they're the ones facing them. Talking about disability not as a tragedy but as a reality that deserves dignity, visibility, and care.

I wasn't trying to inspire.

I was trying to be faithful.

Faithful with the story I'd been given.

Faithful with the breath I still had.

Faithful with the truth that God doesn't preserve lives without intention.

Advocacy didn't erase my limitations.

It gave them direction.

My body might not do everything it once did, but my voice carried weight. My experience had value. My survival could become a bridge instead of a burden.

I hadn't been left here to return to who I was.

I had been left here to walk forward as who I am.

On purpose.

For a purpose.

And for the first time since everything changed, that felt like enough to keep going.

25

Stepping Forward

Purpose doesn't announce itself all at once.

It nudges.

It whispers.

It repeats itself until you finally stop dismissing it as coincidence.

For me, that nudge came in the form of a pageant I had never imagined myself in.

Ms. Wheelchair USA.

At first, it felt almost absurd. A pageant? After everything? I wasn't looking for a crown. I wasn't trying to be seen. I was still learning how to live in a body that drew attention whether I wanted it to or not.

But the more I listened, the clearer it became.

This wasn't about appearance.

It was about platform.

It was about voice.

About advocacy.

About showing up in spaces where disability is often either erased or misunderstood.

I hesitated.

Putting myself forward meant visibility. It meant scrutiny. It meant inviting opinions about my body, my story, my worth. I had spent so long learning how to protect myself by covering scars, choosing when to be seen.

This felt like the opposite.

And yet, I kept coming back to the same truth:

If God had left me here on purpose, then obedience might require visibility.

I didn't step forward because I felt ready.

I stepped forward because I felt called.

The process stretched me in ways I didn't expect. It asked me to articulate my story, not just the miracle parts, but the ongoing realities. The access issues. The assumptions. The quiet exclusions people don't notice until they're the ones navigating them.

I spoke about parking, not as a convenience, but as access.

I spoke about public spaces, not as neutral, but as designed with assumptions.

I spoke about disability, not as something to overcome, but as something that deserves respect.

And slowly, something shifted.

I realized I wasn't standing alone.

I was standing *with* others who had been overlooked. With people whose lives were shaped by barriers most never think about. With a community that didn't need pity, it needed representation.

That year of advocacy changed me.

It gave shape to my purpose.

It sharpened my voice.

It taught me that leadership doesn't require physical strength, it requires courage, consistency, and truth.

I wasn't trying to reclaim my old life.

I was learning how to steward the one I'd been given.

Stepping forward didn't erase fear.

But it clarified calling.

And calling, I was learning, is rarely comfortable, but it is always intentional.

26

Advocacy Becomes A Calling

Advocacy didn't end when the year did.

If anything, it clarified.

What I learned quickly was that a crown can open doors, but it can't do the work for you. Titles fade. Platforms change. But the needs remain, waiting for someone willing to keep showing up when the spotlight moves on.

I began to notice things I hadn't noticed before.

Or maybe I had noticed them but now I had language for them.

Parking spaces misused and dismissed as minor inconveniences. Entrances labeled accessible that still required help to navigate. Well-meaning people who didn't understand that access isn't about preference, it's about dignity.

I started speaking up.

Not angrily.

Not defensively.

But clearly.

I talked about why parking matters. Why "just for a minute" can mean someone doesn't get to participate at all. Why access isn't special treatment, it's equal opportunity to exist in the same spaces everyone else takes for granted.

Sometimes people listened.

Sometimes they didn't.

But I learned that obedience isn't measured by response; it's measured by faithfulness.

Advocacy also required patience. Change doesn't come all at once. It comes through conversations that feel small. Through repetition. Through choosing to educate instead of disengaging.

I shared my story not because it was dramatic but because it was real.

I talked about how a body can change overnight. How independence can disappear without warning. How easy it is to overlook access until you're the one searching for it.

And slowly, something shifted.

People began to see differently.

Not because I convinced them, but because I invited them to imagine life from a seat they had never occupied.

Advocacy stopped being something I *did* and became something I *was*.

Not because I had all the answers.

But because I was willing to stay present in the questions.

I was no longer trying to return to who I had been.

I was walking forward as someone shaped by suffering, sustained by faith, and committed to leaving spaces better than I found them.

God hadn't left me here by accident.

He had entrusted me with perspective.

And perspective, when offered with humility and truth, can change more than policies.

It can change hearts.

27

No Longer Hiding

For a long time, being seen felt like a threat.

Not because I didn't believe in my purpose, but because I remembered how vulnerable it felt when my body told a story I hadn't yet learned how to carry. The helmet. The wheelchair. The scars. The assumptions. The fear that people would decide who I was before I ever spoke.

I learned how to protect myself in those early days.

I chose when to go out.

I chose what to wear.

I chose when to explain and when to stay quiet.

Those choices mattered. They helped me survive a season when everything felt exposed.

But seasons change.

Somewhere along the way, I realized I wasn't hiding anymore, I was *ready*.

Ready to let my body be what it was without apology.

Ready to let my story be visible without needing to soften it.

Ready to trust that God's purpose didn't depend on how comfortable I felt.

Visibility stopped feeling like vulnerability and started feeling like obedience.

Not loud.

Not performative.

Just honest.

I no longer needed to prove that I was mentally capable, spiritually strong, or emotionally resilient. I didn't need to overexplain my faith or justify my limitations.

I was enough as I was.

Disability didn't make me less faithful.

Dependence didn't make me less strong.

Being changed didn't mean being diminished.

I began to notice something else, too.

When I stopped shrinking myself, others stopped shrinking away.

Conversations deepened. Stories were shared. People admitted fears they had never voiced. Struggles they had hidden because they didn't know where to place them.

My scars didn't repel people.

They invited honesty.

I wasn't leading because I had everything figured out.

I was leading because I was willing to be seen *as I was*, still walking with a cane, still limited, still learning, still trusting.

And in that space, fear loosened its grip.

Not because life became easier, but because I no longer carried it alone.

God hadn't healed me back into invisibility.

He had healed me into presence.

And presence, I was learning, is one of the most powerful forms of witness there is.

28

If I Had Gone to Sleep

There are moments I return to more than others.

Not because they haunt me but because they clarify everything.

I think about that night.

The football game playing softly in the background.

The recliner.

The headache I had learned to live with.

I think about how easy it would have been to stay quiet.

To shrug it off.

To go to sleep.

To assume morning would fix what felt inconvenient instead of catastrophic.

If I had gone to sleep, I likely wouldn't be here.

If my husband hadn't walked in.

If he hadn't recognized the signs.

If he hadn't insisted when I protested.

If one decision had gone differently, this book wouldn't exist. My children's lives would look different. My grandchild(ren) would grow up without knowing me the way they do now.

The truth is uncomfortable, but it's also sacred.

Life is fragile in ways we don't like to think about until we're forced to.

I don't share this to create fear.

I share it to create awareness.

Because strokes don't always announce themselves loudly.

Because suffering doesn't always look dramatic.

Because sometimes the most important moments are the quiet ones we're tempted to dismiss.

Looking back, I see God's hand not just in the miracle moments but in the ordinary ones. In a husband coming inside at just the right time. In a phone call made despite resistance. In help delayed by weather but not denied by purpose.

God didn't just save my life.

He positioned it.

Positioned it for conversations I never planned to have.

For advocacy I never imagined leading.

For faith that had to deepen because it could no longer rely on comfort.

I don't know what moments you might be tempted to dismiss in your own life.

The pain you've normalized.

The fatigue you've explained away.

The calling you've postponed because the timing doesn't feel right.

But I know this:

If God has kept you here, it is not without intention.

You don't need a platform to live on purpose.

You don't need a miracle story to matter.

You don't need to be fully healed to be fully faithful.

You just need to stay awake to the life you've been given.

Because sometimes, the most faithful thing you can do is not go to sleep.

29

Even Now

I used to think surrender was something you did once.

A single moment.

A clear decision.

A line crossed and never revisited.

I know better now.

Surrender is something you return to, again and again, especially when life doesn't resolve the way you hoped it would.

Even now.

Even now, my body carries limits.

Even now, my hand remains still.

Even now, I walk with a cane and plan my days differently than I once did.

Even now, there are moments of grief that surface without warning, when I realize what I won't do the way I once imagined.

And even now, there is goodness.

Not because everything was restored.

But because I was.

Restored to purpose.

Restored to presence.

Restored to a faith that no longer depends on outcomes to be real.

God did not rush my healing.

He did not explain every loss.

He did not give me back the life I had before.

He gave me something deeper.

He gave me Himself—steady, near, faithful in ways I hadn't known how to recognize before.

I am not here because I was strong.

I am here because I was held.

Held through surgeries I don't remember.

Held through prayers I couldn't form.

Held through seasons where survival felt like enough and purpose felt far away.

And slowly, patiently, that purpose took shape.

Not as a spotlight.

Not as perfection.

But as obedience.

Writing.

Advocating.

Speaking when silence would have been easier.

Showing up when hiding felt safer.

If you've read this far, maybe part of my story has brushed against yours.

Maybe you're living in a body that has changed.

Maybe your faith has been tested by unanswered questions.

Maybe you're still grieving what didn't return, even as you're grateful for what did.

If so, hear this clearly:

You are not behind.

You are not forgotten.

You are not disqualified by limitation.

Purpose does not require wholeness.

Calling does not wait for comfort.

God does not waste what hurts.

Even now, right where you are, He is present.

And if He has kept you here, it is not by accident.

It is on purpose.

For a purpose.

Not always loud.

Not always visible.

But always meaningful.

This story doesn't end with everything fixed.

It ends with everything entrusted.

And that, finally, has been enough.

Dear Reader,

If you're holding this book, it means you stayed.

You stayed through fear, uncertainty, loss, and the slow work of becoming. That tells me something about you—you're not afraid of honesty, even when it's uncomfortable.

I didn't write this story to offer answers or formulas. I wrote it because life doesn't always resolve neatly, and faith doesn't require pretending that it does.

If you are reading this while living in a changed body, a changed season, or a changed version of yourself— please know this: you are not alone, and you are not forgotten.

God's presence is not measured by what returns to us, but by what sustains us when it doesn't.

My hope is that somewhere in these pages, you felt seen. That you felt permission to grieve honestly, trust deeply, and surrender repeatedly—without shame.

If God can use my story, He can use yours.

Even now.

With gratitude,

Amy

A Closing Prayer

God,

Thank You for the gift of life—especially when it doesn't look the way we expected.

Thank You for presence that doesn't depend on outcomes, and faith that holds us when answers don't come.

For those reading this who are tired, grieving, or afraid, meet them gently.

For those learning to live in changed bodies or altered dreams, remind them that purpose has not passed them by.

Teach us how to surrender again and again—not in defeat, but in trust.

Help us to see that being kept here is not an accident, but an invitation.

May we live on purpose, for Your purpose, even now.

Amen.

Faith Reflection & Discussion Questions

These questions are designed for personal reflection, book clubs, or faith groups.

1. Where in your life have you been tempted to believe that "different" means "less than"?

2. How has suffering changed the way you understand surrender?

3. What does it look like for you to trust God without knowing the outcome?

4. Have you ever felt pressure to "move on" before you were ready? How did that affect you?

5. In what ways might God be inviting you to live more visibly or more honestly?

6. What does purpose look like in your current season—not a future one?

FORWARD
From Signs to Strength

BE FAST:
Know the signs of a stroke

I didn't know the signs of a stroke when it happened to me. I didn't know what my body was trying to say, or how quickly everything could change. What I know now, I wish I had known then.

If you remember nothing else from my story, remember this: strokes are medical emergencies, and minutes matter. The BE FAST method is a simple way to recognize the warning signs and respond quickly. This page exists because awareness saves lives—and because I don't want anyone else to learn these signs the hard way.

B: Balance - Sudden loss of balance, coordination, or dizziness. A person may have trouble walking, feel unusually unsteady, or appear disoriented without warning.

E: Eyes - Sudden changes in vision in one or both eyes. This may include blurred vision, double vision, or loss of vision altogether.

F: Face - Face drooping or numbness, often on one side. Ask the person to smile. If one side of the face droops or does not move the same as the other, this is a warning sign.

A: Arms - Arm or leg weakness or numbness, especially on one side of the body. Ask the person to raise both arms. If one arm drifts downward or cannot be lifted, take it seriously.

S: Speech - Slurred speech, difficulty speaking, or trouble understanding words. Ask the person to repeat a simple sentence. If speech is unclear or incorrect, this may indicate a stroke.

T: Time - Time to call **911 immediately**. Do not wait. Do not drive yourself. Every minute matters when it comes to stroke treatment and recovery.

If you notice any of these signs, even if they come and go, call 911 right away.

Final Word

If this book resonated with you, I would be honored if you would leave a review. Reviews help stories like this reach readers who may need them at exactly the right moment.

More importantly, if even one person feels less alone, more seen, or more hopeful because you shared this story forward, then this journey continues to matter.

Thank you for reading.

Thank you for staying.

This is a story for anyone navigating loss, chronic illness, disability, or faith tested by unanswered questions. It is a reminder that purpose does not require wholeness, surrender is ongoing, and God wastes nothing, even now.

A Word About Salvation

Throughout this book, you've read about survival, surrender, and purpose.

But the greatest truth woven through every page is not my story.

It's God's.

The same God who held me through surgeries, uncertainty, and loss is the God who offers something even greater than physical healing: **new life in Christ**.

If you are reading this and feel stirred, curious, or quietly drawn toward God, I want you to know that faith does not begin with having everything figured out.

It begins with surrender.

The Gospel, Simply

The Bible tells us that every person has fallen short of God's perfect standard.

"For all have sinned and fall short of the glory of God."

— Romans 3:23

Sin separates us from God — not just in actions, but in nature. And no amount of good works, effort, or intention can bridge that gap.

"For the wages of sin is death, but the gift of God is eternal life in Christ Jesus our Lord."

— Romans 6:23

God did not leave us separated.

Out of love, He sent His Son, Jesus Christ, to take our place.

"But God demonstrates His own love toward us, in that while we were still sinners, Christ died for us."

— Romans 5:8

Jesus lived a sinless life, died on the cross for our sins, and rose again — defeating sin and death once and for all.

Salvation is not earned.

It is received.

"For by grace you have been saved through faith, and that not of yourselves; it is the gift of God."

— Ephesians 2:8–9

What It Means to Believe

Believing in Jesus is more than intellectual agreement.

It is trusting Him as Savior and surrendering to Him as Lord.

"If you confess with your mouth the Lord Jesus and believe in your heart that God has raised Him from the dead, you will be saved."

— Romans 10:9

This doesn't mean life suddenly becomes easy.

It means you are no longer alone.

It means forgiveness, new identity, and eternal hope — beginning now.

What Comes Next

Salvation is the beginning, not the end.

If you have prayed this prayer or are considering faith:

• tell someone, including me. Reach out to me on my Facebook page https://www.facebook.com/thescarstellthestory

• read God's Word regularly

• find a Bible believing and preaching church

• surround yourself with believers who will walk with you

And know this:

God does not ask you to have everything healed, whole, or resolved before coming to Him.

He meets you exactly where you are.

Even now.

A Prayer of Surrender

If you desire to place your faith in Jesus, you can pray something like this:

> God,
>
> I know that I am a sinner and that I cannot save myself. I believe that Jesus died for my sins and rose again. I turn from my sin and place my trust in Him alone.
>
> Jesus, I surrender my life to You. Be my Savior and my Lord. Thank You for Your grace and for new life in You.
>
> Amen.